POWER BLENDS

75 Recipes for the Nutri Ninja® Ninja® BlendMax DUO™

Editors and Content: Meghan Reilly, Kenzie Swanhart, Elizabeth Skladany, and Daniel Davis

Recipe Development: Amy Golino, Corey Mota, Judy Cannon, and Great Flavors Recipe Development Team

Design and Layout: Talia Mangeym

Copywriter: Melissa Stefanini

Creative Director: Lauren Wiernasz

Photo Direction: Lauren Wiernasz and Talia Mangeym

Photography: Michael Piazza and Quentin Bacon

Published in the United States of America by
SharkNinja Operating LLC
180 Wells Avenue
Newton, MA 02459

BL2010 ISBN: 978-1-5323-0657-0

Ninja and Nutri Ninja are registered trademarks of SharkNinja Operating LLC.
Auto-iQ, BlendMax DUO, Ninjaccino, and Smooth Boost are trademarks of SharkNinja Operating LLC.

10   9   8   7   6   5   4   3   2   1

Printed in China

MEET YOUR GREATEST LIQUID ASSET.

Whether it's drinks for you or a whole crew, your Nutri Ninja® Ninja® BlendMax DUO™ will power through all your thirst-quenching needs. We pushed pitcher capacity and blade speed to the max. Then, we pumped up the motor with 2 horsepower of pure blending muscle. So the only thing you ever have to worry about is choosing a recipe.

TABLE
OF
CONTENTS

18

CRANBERRY
OAT
SOOTHER

24

57

CREAMY
BUTTERNUT
SQUASH
SAUCE

64

AVOCADO
WATERCRESS
SALAD DRESSING

71

107

ROCKY
ROAD
MILKSHAKE

101

PUT IT IN SMOOTH CONTROL.

Ninja® has set a new standard in drink and meal customization. Auto-iQ™ Smooth Boost™ gives you the power to control the texture and consistency of everything from nutritious juices and smoothies to delectable dips and desserts, all at the touch of a button.

SMOOTHIE

Using frozen fruit? Select **BOOST YES** for the smoothest results. If you're sticking to fresh fruit, you're all set with **BOOST NO**.

TO BOOST OR NOT TO BOOST?

Selecting BOOST YES or BOOST NO adds just the right amount of pulses and pauses to get the results you want from each recipe. Here's how to get the most out of each program on your Nutri Ninja® Ninja® BlendMax DUO™.

PUREE

Purees are a varied bunch. Choose **BOOST YES** for a smooth puree; choose **BOOST NO** for a chunkier texture.

FROZEN DRINK

Select **BOOST YES** for a creamier consistency. If you prefer a slushy-like finish, select **BOOST NO**.

EXTRACT

Select **BOOST YES** if your recipe includes fibrous ingredients with skins and seeds. Otherwise, use **BOOST NO**.

TOTAL CRUSH

Use Total Crush for ice-based treats; select **BOOST YES** for a fine, snow-like consistency, and choose **BOOST NO** for a chunkier, yet even crush.

LOAD IT UP.

It's time to take your Nutri Ninja® Ninja® BlendMax Duo™ for a spin.
When it comes to loading the containers, order is everything.
Use these quick tips and visual guide to ensure your recipes
turn out just the way you want them, every time.

Don't overfill the Nutri Ninja® cups.
If you feel resistance when attaching
the Pro Extractor Blades® Assembly
to the cup, remove some ingredients.

When loading the
Total Crushing® Pitcher,
do not exceed the
max fill line.

CAUTION: Remove the Pro Extractor Blades® Assembly from the Nutri Ninja® cup upon completion of blending.
Do not store ingredients before or after blending in the cup with the blade assembly attached. Some foods may contain
active ingredients or release gases that will expand if left in a sealed container, resulting in excessive pressure buildup
that can pose a risk of injury. For ingredient storage, only use Spout Lid to cover.

5 Top off with ice or frozen ingredients.

4 Next add any dry or sticky ingredients like seeds, powders, and nut butters.

3 Pour in liquid or yogurt next.

For thinner results or a juice-like drink, add more liquid as desired.

2 Next add leafy greens and herbs.

START FROM THE BOTTOM UP

1 Start by adding fresh fruits and vegetables.

(Note: For best results, cut ingredients in 1-inch chunks. Do not place frozen ingredients first in the Nutri Ninja® cups).

BUILD THE PERFECT SMOOTHIE.

The perfect smoothie is a sum of its parts. Choose an ingredient from each column for the most delicious results.

CHOOSE YOUR BASE

Almond milk

Coconut milk

Rice milk

Soy milk

Fresh juice

Chilled green tea

Coconut water

Maple water

Water

CHOOSE YOUR FRUIT

Apples

Bananas

Blackberries

Blueberries

Raspberries

Strawberries

Cherries

Kiwis

Mangoes

Oranges

Peaches

Pineapple

MAKE IT GREEN

Kale

Spinach

Watercress

Cabbage

Celery

Cucumber

Fresh mint

MAKE IT THICK & CREAMY

Avocado

Chia seeds

Coconut

Greek yogurt

Ice

Nut butter

Nuts

Oats

BOOST IT UP A NOTCH

Bee pollen

Cacao powder

Cinnamon

Coconut oil

Ginger root

Flaxseed

Protein powder

Maca powder

Matcha powder

Spirulina

Turmeric

ADD A LITTLE SWEETNESS

Agave nectar

Dates

Figs

Honey

Maple syrup

Vanilla extract

Stevia

PEAR & HIBISCUS TEA SMOOTHIE

Prep time: 5 minutes
Container: 24-ounce Tritan™ Nutri Ninja® Cup
Makes: 2 (9-ounce) servings

INGREDIENTS

½ pear, cored, chopped

½ lemon, peeled, seeds removed

½ cup spinach

1 cup brewed hibiscus tea, chilled

2 teaspoons honey

¾ cup ice

DIRECTIONS

1. Place all ingredients into the 24-ounce Tritan Nutri Ninja Cup in the order listed.

2. Select BOOST YES Auto-iQ™ SMOOTHIE.

3. Remove blades from cup after blending.

DO NOT BLEND HOT INGREDIENTS.

STRAWBERRY MELON BLAST

Prep time: 5 minutes
Container: 24-ounce Tritan™ Nutri Ninja® Cup
Makes: 1 (12-ounce) serving

INGREDIENTS

¼ medium cucumber, peeled, cut in half

4 strawberries, hulled

¾ cup cantaloupe chunks

¼ cup ice

DIRECTIONS

1. Place all ingredients into the 24-ounce Tritan Nutri Ninja Cup in the order listed.

2. Select BOOST YES Auto-iQ™ SMOOTHIE.

3. Remove blades from cup after blending.

APPLE
ALMOND
SUPER JUICE

Prep time: 5 minutes
Container: 24-ounce Tritan™ Nutri Ninja® Cup
Makes: 2 (8-ounce) servings

INGREDIENTS

1 green apple, peeled, cut in half

$\frac{1}{2}$ small ripe banana, cut in half

1 cup unsweetened almond milk

1 tablespoon almond butter

1 tablespoon white chia seeds

1 scoop protein powder

$\frac{1}{2}$ cup ice

DIRECTIONS

1. Place all ingredients into the 24-ounce Tritan Nutri Ninja Cup in the order listed.

2. Select BOOST YES Auto-iQ™ SMOOTHIE.

3. Remove blades from cup after blending.

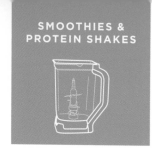

APPLE PIE SMOOTHIE

Prep time: 5 minutes
Container: 88-ounce Blender Pitcher
Makes: 8 (8-ounce) servings

INGREDIENTS

4 large Golden Delicious apples, cored, chopped

1 tablespoon lemon juice

4 cups unsweetened almond milk

2 tablespoons brown sugar

1 teaspoon ground cinnamon

$\frac{1}{4}$ teaspoon ground nutmeg

$\frac{1}{2}$ teaspoon salt

4 cups ice

DIRECTIONS

1. Place all ingredients into the 88-ounce Blender Pitcher in the order listed.

2. Select BOOST YES Auto-iQ™ SMOOTHIE.

BLENDING SUGGESTION

To break down the apple skins as finely as possible, we like to use BOOST Yes.

STRAWBERRY BANANA PROTEIN SHAKE

Prep time: 5 minutes
Container: 88-ounce Blender Pitcher
Makes: 7 (10-ounce) servings

INGREDIENTS

3 small ripe bananas

2 ½ cups coconut water

2 ½ cups fat-free Greek yogurt

5 scoops protein powder

5 cups frozen strawberries

DIRECTIONS

1. Place all ingredients into the 88-ounce Blender Pitcher in the order listed.

2. Select BOOST YES Auto-iQ™ SMOOTHIE.

CHOCOLATE PROTEIN POWER

Prep time: 5 minutes
Container: 88-ounce Blender Pitcher
Makes: 8 (8-ounce) servings

INGREDIENTS

2 ripe bananas, cut in half

4 cups 1% milk

3 scoops chocolate protein powder

½ cup peanut butter

3 tablespoons cocoa powder

3 cups ice

DIRECTIONS

1. Place all ingredients into the 88-ounce Blender Pitcher in the order listed.

2. Select BOOST NO Auto-iQ™ SMOOTHIE.

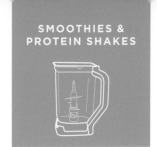

GRASSHOPPER SMOOTHIE

Prep time: 5 minutes
Container: 88-ounce Blender Pitcher
Makes: 9 (8-ounce) servings

INGREDIENTS

2 frozen ripe bananas

5 cups spinach leaves

4 cups almond milk

¼ cup fresh mint leaves

2 cups ice

DIRECTIONS

1. Place all ingredients into the 88-ounce Blender Pitcher in the order listed.

2. Select BOOST YES Auto-iQ™ SMOOTHIE.

CRANBERRY OAT SOOTHER

Prep time: 5 minutes
Container: 24-ounce Tritan™ Nutri Ninja® Cup
Makes: 2 (10-ounce) servings

INGREDIENTS

½ cup walnut pieces

⅓ cup whole-berry cranberry sauce

1 cup oat milk

¼ teaspoon vanilla

1 tablespoon honey

Dash salt

1 ½ cups ice

DIRECTIONS

1. Place all ingredients into the 24-ounce Tritan Nutri Ninja Cup in the order listed.

2. Select BOOST YES Auto-iQ™ SMOOTHIE.

3. Remove blades from cup after blending.

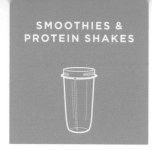

VANILLA MATCHA SHAKE

Prep time: 5 minutes
Container: 24-ounce Tritan™ Nutri Ninja® Cup
Makes: 2 (12-ounce) servings

INGREDIENTS

1 cup vanilla oat milk

1 teaspoon lime juice

1 scoop vanilla protein powder

2 teaspoons matcha powder

Dash salt

1 cup ice

DIRECTIONS

1. Place all ingredients into the 24-ounce Tritan Nutri Ninja Cup in the order listed.

2. Select BOOST NO Auto-iQ™ SMOOTHIE.

3. Remove blades from cup after blending.

BERRY
PEPITA
SMOOTHIE

Prep time: 4 minutes
Container: 24-ounce Tritan™ Nutri Ninja® Cup
Makes: 2 (10-ounce) servings

INGREDIENTS

1 cup strawberries, hulled

1 cup milk

2 tablespoons pepita seeds

1 tablespoon agave nectar

1 cup ice

DIRECTIONS

1. Place all ingredients into the 24-ounce Tritan Nutri Ninja
   Cup in the order listed.

2. Select BOOST NO Auto-iQ™ SMOOTHIE.

3. Remove blades from cup after blending.

ISLAND SUNRISE SMOOTHIE

Prep time: 5 minutes
Container: 24-ounce Tritan™ Nutri Ninja® Cup
Makes: 2 (12-ounce) servings

INGREDIENTS

$^3/_4$ cup pineapple chunks

1 small ripe banana

1 $^1/_4$ cups coconut water

$^3/_4$ cup frozen strawberries

$^3/_4$ cup frozen mango chunks

DIRECTIONS

1. Place all ingredients into the 24-ounce Tritan Nutri Ninja Cup in the order listed.

2. Select BOOST YES Auto-iQ™ SMOOTHIE.

3. Remove blades from cup after blending.

GINGER-ADE

Prep time: 5 minutes
Container: 24-ounce Tritan™ Nutri Ninja® Cup
Makes: 3 (8-ounce) servings

INGREDIENTS

1-inch piece fresh ginger, peeled

2 lemons, peeled, cut in quarters, seeds removed

1 ¾ cups water

3 tablespoons agave nectar

1 cup ice

DIRECTIONS

1. Place all ingredients into the 24-ounce Tritan Nutri Ninja Cup in the order listed.

2. Select BOOST YES Auto-iQ™ EXTRACT.

3. Remove blades from cup after blending.

HONEY CITRUS SUNSHINE

Prep time: 5 minutes
Container: 24-ounce Tritan™ Nutri Ninja® Cup
Makes: 2 (11-ounce) servings

INGREDIENTS

1 orange, peeled,
cut in half, seeds removed

1 grapefruit, peeled,
cut in half, seeds removed

2 mandarins, peeled

½ cup water

1 tablespoon honey

1 cup ice

DIRECTIONS

1. Place all ingredients into the 24-ounce Tritan Nutri Ninja Cup in the order listed.

2. Select BOOST YES Auto-iQ™ SMOOTHIE.

3. Remove blades from cup after blending.

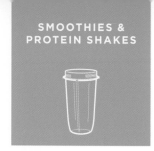

KALE PINEAPPLE MINT

Prep time: 5 minutes
Container: 24-ounce Tritan™ Nutri Ninja® Cup
Makes: 2 (7-ounce) servings

INGREDIENTS

1 cup pineapple chunks

½ small ripe banana

⅓ cup baby spinach

⅓ cup kale leaves

1 tablespoon fresh mint leaves

½ cup coconut water

½ cup ice

DIRECTIONS

1. Place all ingredients into the 24-ounce Tritan Nutri Ninja Cup in the order listed.

2. Select BOOST YES Auto-iQ™ EXTRACT.

3. Remove blades from cup after blending.

COOL CANTALOUPE CUCUMBER

Prep time: 5 minutes
Container: 24-ounce Tritan™ Nutri Ninja® Cup
Makes: 2 (9-ounce) servings

INGREDIENTS

1/2 medium cucumber, unpeeled, cut in 1-inch chunks

1 cup cantaloupe chunks

3/4 cup pineapple chunks

1/2 cup water

1/2 cup ice

DIRECTIONS

1. Place all ingredients into the 24-ounce Tritan Nutri Ninja Cup in the order listed.

2. Select BOOST YES Auto-iQ™ EXTRACT.

3. Remove blades from cup after blending.

SWEET CUCUMBER BASIL

Prep time: 5 minutes
Container: 24-ounce Tritan™ Nutri Ninja® Cup
Makes: 2 (10-ounce) servings

INGREDIENTS

4-inch piece English cucumber

½ green apple, unpeeled, cored, cut in half

2 tablespoons fresh basil

1 cup frozen green seedless grapes

1 cup water

DIRECTIONS

1. Place all ingredients into the 24-ounce Tritan Nutri Ninja Cup in the order listed.

2. Select BOOST YES Auto-iQ™ EXTRACT.

3. Remove blades from cup after blending.

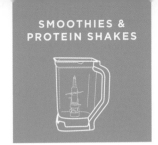

THE RED DRAGON

Prep time: 5 minutes
Container: 88-ounce Blender Pitcher
Makes: 9 (8-ounce) servings

INGREDIENTS

3 cups strawberries, hulled

1 red dragon fruit, peeled,
cut in half

4 cups almond milk

2 cups frozen mango chunks

DIRECTIONS

1. Place all ingredients into the 88-ounce Blender Pitcher in the order listed.

2. Select BOOST YES Auto-iQ™ SMOOTHIE.

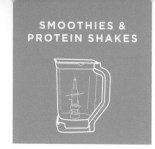

WATERMELON QUENCH

Prep time: 5 minutes
Container: 88-ounce Blender Pitcher
Makes: 4 (8-ounce) servings

INGREDIENTS

2 ½ cups watermelon chunks

2 cups pomegranate juice

1 cup frozen peaches

DIRECTIONS

1. Place all ingredients into the 88-ounce Blender Pitcher in the order listed.

2. Select BOOST YES Auto-iQ™ SMOOTHIE.

PREP SUGGESTION

During the summer months, stock up on seasonal fruit, then cut and freeze it for your wintertime smoothies.

PB JAMMER

Prep time: 4 minutes
Container: 24-ounce Tritan™ Nutri Ninja® Cup
Makes: 2 (10-ounce) servings

INGREDIENTS

1 ½ cups strawberries, hulled

1 small frozen ripe banana

¾ cup milk

2 tablespoons peanut butter

½ cup ice

DIRECTIONS

1. Place all ingredients into the 24-ounce Tritan Nutri Ninja Cup in the order listed.

2. Select BOOST NO Auto-iQ™ SMOOTHIE.

3. Remove blades from cup after blending.

CHOCO-LOCO

Prep time: 4 minutes
Container: 24-ounce Tritan™ Nutri Ninja® Cup
Makes: 2 (8-ounce) servings

INGREDIENTS

1 small frozen ripe banana

1 cup chocolate almond milk

½ cup old fashioned rolled oats

1 tablespoon cocoa powder

2 tablespoons chocolate chips

½ cup ice

DIRECTIONS

1. Place all ingredients into the 24-ounce Tritan Nutri Ninja Cup in the order listed.

2. Select BOOST YES Auto-iQ™ SMOOTHIE.

3. Remove blades from cup after blending.

COOL GINGER PEAR

Prep time: 5 minutes
Container: 24-ounce Tritan™ Nutri Ninja® Cup
Makes: 2 (9-ounce) servings

INGREDIENTS

1 ripe pear, cored, cut in quarters

$\frac{1}{4}$-inch piece fresh ginger, peeled

2 teaspoons fresh lemon juice

2 $\frac{1}{4}$ cups cold water

Honey, to taste

DIRECTIONS

1. Place all ingredients into the 24-ounce Tritan Nutri Ninja Cup in the order listed.

2. Select BOOST YES Auto-iQ™ EXTRACT.

3. Remove blades from cup after blending.

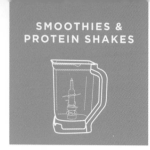

MANGO-NANA

Prep time: 5 minutes
Container: 88-ounce Blender Pitcher
Makes: 7 (8-ounce) servings

INGREDIENTS

2 ripe bananas

2 cups mango nectar

1 cup milk

1 tablespoon honey

3 cups frozen mango chunks

2 cups ice

DIRECTIONS

1. Place all ingredients into the 88-ounce Blender Pitcher in the order listed.

2. Select BOOST YES Auto-iQ™ FROZEN DRINK.

PINEAPPLE PEAR COLADA

Prep time: 5 minutes
Container: 88-ounce Blender Pitcher
Makes: 7 (8-ounce) servings

INGREDIENTS

3 pears, peeled, cored,
cut in quarters

2 cups pineapple chunks

1 can (13.5 ounces)
light coconut milk

$\frac{1}{2}$ cup coconut water

4 cups ice

DIRECTIONS

1. Place all ingredients into the 88-ounce Blender Pitcher in the order listed.

2. Select BOOST YES Auto-iQ™ SMOOTHIE.

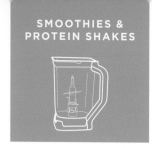

CHOCOLATE CHERRY PROTEIN BLAST

Prep time: 5 minutes
Container: 88-ounce Blender Pitcher
Makes: 6 (8-ounce) servings

INGREDIENTS

1 ½ ripe avocados,
pits removed, peeled

2 ½ cups unsweetened
almond milk

2 ½ teaspoons unsweetened
cocoa powder

2 scoops chocolate
protein powder

2 cups frozen cherries

DIRECTIONS

1. Place all ingredients into the 88-ounce Blender Pitcher in the order listed.

2. Select BOOST YES Auto-iQ™ SMOOTHIE.

PISTACHIO YOGURT SMOOTHIE

Prep time: 4 minutes
Container: 24-ounce Tritan™ Nutri Ninja® Cup
Makes: 3 (8-ounce) servings

INGREDIENTS

¾ cup 1% milk

¾ cup nonfat Greek yogurt

2 tablespoons apricot preserves

1 scoop vanilla protein powder

2 tablespoons pistachios

¼ teaspoon ground cinnamon

¾ cup ice

DIRECTIONS

1. Place all ingredients into the 24-ounce Tritan Nutri Ninja Cup in the order listed.

2. Select BOOST YES Auto-iQ™ SMOOTHIE.

3. Remove blades from cup after blending.

CREAMY FRENCH ONION SOUP

Prep time: 15 minutes **Cook time:** 30 minutes
Container: 88-ounce Blender Pitcher
Makes: 7 (8-ounce) servings

INGREDIENTS

3 tablespoons unsalted butter

2 cloves garlic, chopped

3 large onions, chopped

$1/3$ cup all-purpose flour

2 teaspoons salt

1 teaspoon ground black pepper

6 cups low-sodium
vegetable broth

6 slices French bread,
cut 1-inch thick

DIRECTIONS

1. Place butter, garlic, and onions into a 5-quart saucepan over medium low heat. Cook for 5 minutes.

2. Add flour, salt, and pepper to saucepan. Stir to incorporate. Add broth and bring to a boil. Reduce heat to medium-low and cook for 20 minutes.

3. Remove from heat and cool to room temperature.

4. Place cooled mixture and bread into the 88-ounce Blender Pitcher. Select BOOST YES Auto-iQ™ PUREE.

5. Return soup to saucepan, then simmer until heated through.

DO NOT BLEND HOT INGREDIENTS.

SMOKY BLACK BEAN SOUP

Prep time: 15 minutes **Cook time:** 35 minutes
Container: 88-ounce Blender Pitcher
Makes: 9 (8-ounce) servings

INGREDIENTS

1 tablespoon canola oil

2 cloves garlic,
peeled, chopped

1 large onion, chopped

1 red bell pepper,
seeds removed, chopped

2 cans (15 ounces each)
black beans, rinsed, drained

1 can (14.5 ounces)
diced tomatoes

2 tablespoons smoked paprika

1 tablespoon ground cumin

2 teaspoons salt

1 teaspoon ground black pepper

6 cups low-sodium
vegetable broth

DIRECTIONS

1. Place oil, garlic, and onion into a 5-quart saucepan over medium-low heat. Cook for 5 minutes.

2. Add remaining ingredients to saucepan and bring to a boil. Reduce heat to medium-low and cook for 25 minutes.

3. Remove from heat and cool to room temperature.

4. Place cooled mixture into the 88-ounce Blender Pitcher. Select BOOST NO Auto-iQ™ PUREE.

5. Return soup to saucepan, then simmer until heated through.

DO NOT BLEND HOT INGREDIENTS.

CAULIFLOWER CHEDDAR SOUP

Prep time: 15 minutes **Cook time:** 30 minutes
Container: 88-ounce Blender Pitcher
Makes: 9 (8-ounce) servings

INGREDIENTS

3 tablespoons unsalted butter

2 cloves garlic, peeled, chopped

1 large onion, chopped

$1/3$ cup all-purpose flour

2 teaspoons salt

1 teaspoon ground black pepper

1 large head cauliflower,
cut into florets

5 cups low-sodium
vegetable broth

2 cups shredded cheddar cheese

2 cups milk

DIRECTIONS

1. Add butter, garlic, and onion to a 5-quart saucepan over medium-low heat. Cook for 5 minutes.

2. Add flour, salt, and pepper to saucepan. Stir to combine. Add cauliflower and broth. Bring to a boil, then reduce heat to medium-low and cook for 20 minutes.

3. Remove soup from heat and cool to room temperature.

4. Place cooled mixture into the 88-ounce Blender Pitcher. Select BOOST YES Auto-iQ™ PUREE.

5. Return soup to saucepan. Add cheese and milk, then simmer until cheese is melted and soup is heated through.

DO NOT BLEND HOT INGREDIENTS.

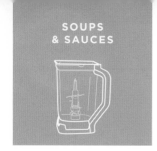

TURKEY WILD RICE CHOWDER

Prep time: 15 minutes **Cook time:** 35 minutes
Container: 88-ounce Blender Pitcher
Makes: 6 (8-ounce) servings

INGREDIENTS

3 tablespoons unsalted butter

2 cloves garlic, peeled, chopped

1 large onion, chopped

2 stalks celery, chopped

2 medium carrots, peeled, chopped

1/3 cup all-purpose flour

1 tablespoon poultry seasoning

1 1/2 teaspoons salt

1 teaspoon ground black pepper

6 cups low-sodium turkey broth

2 cups cooked wild rice

1 pound cooked turkey breast, diced

DIRECTIONS

1. Place butter, garlic, onions, celery, and carrot into a 5-quart saucepan over medium heat. Cook for 10 minutes.

2. Add flour, poultry seasoning, salt, and pepper to saucepan. Stir to incorporate. Add broth and bring to a boil, then reduce heat to medium-low and cook 20 minutes.

3. Remove from heat and cool to room temperature.

4. Place cooled mixture into the 88-ounce Blender Pitcher. Select BOOST NO Auto-iQ™ PUREE.

5. Return soup to saucepan. Add rice and turkey, then simmer until heated through.

DO NOT BLEND HOT INGREDIENTS.

CITRUS TURKEY BRINE

Prep time: 10 minutes
Container: 88-ounce Blender Pitcher
Makes: 8 ½ cups

INGREDIENTS

6 cups water

1 orange, peeled

1 lemon, peeled

1 medium onion, cut in half

1 cup light brown sugar

³/₄ cup salt

4 cloves garlic, peeled

1 tablespoon ground
black pepper

½ teaspoon ground allspice

DIRECTIONS

1. Place all ingredients into the 88-ounce Blender Pitcher.
2. Select BOOST NO Auto-iQ™ PUREE.

CURRIED CARROT SOUP

Prep time: 15 minutes **Cook time:** 35 minutes
Container: 24-ounce Tritan™ Nutri Ninja® Cup
Makes: 2 (12-ounce) servings

INGREDIENTS

2 teaspoons extra-virgin olive oil

2 cloves garlic, peeled, chopped

1/2 medium yellow onion, chopped

1 teaspoon red curry paste

1 1/2 cups carrots, peeled, chopped

1 1/4 cups low-sodium chicken broth

1 cup light coconut milk

Salt and pepper, to taste

DIRECTIONS

1. Heat oil in a medium saucepan and sauté garlic and onion until translucent, about 3 to 5 minutes.

2. Add red curry paste, carrots, and chicken broth to saucepan; bring to a boil. Reduce heat and simmer until carrots are fork-tender, about 20 to 25 minutes.

3. Remove from heat, add coconut milk, and cool to room temperature.

4. Working in 2 batches, ladle half the cooled mixture into the 24-ounce Tritan Nutri Ninja Cup.

5. Select BOOST NO Auto-iQ™ PUREE. Repeat with remaining soup. Remove blades from cup after blending. Return soup to saucepan and simmer until heated through. Season with salt and pepper to taste.

DO NOT BLEND HOT INGREDIENTS.

**SERVING
SUGGESTION**

This twist on a classic
is gluten and dairy free.
Serve with rice or
wilted spinach.

KICK-IT-UP TOMATO SOUP

Prep time: 10 minutes **Cook time:** 30 minutes
Container: 24-ounce Tritan™ Nutri Ninja® Cup
Makes: 3 (8-ounce) servings

INGREDIENTS

2 teaspoons canola oil

2 cloves garlic, peeled, chopped

¼ medium onion, chopped

½ cup raw cashews

1 can (14.5 ounces)
petite diced tomatoes

1 teaspoon salt

½ teaspoon ground black pepper

½ teaspoon dried basil

1 cup low-sodium
vegetable broth

DIRECTIONS

1. Place oil, garlic, and onions into a 5-quart saucepan over medium-low heat. Cook for 5 minutes.

2. Add remaining ingredients to saucepan and bring to a boil. Reduce heat to medium-low and cook for 20 minutes.

3. Remove from heat and cool to room temperature.

4. Place cooled mixture into the 24-ounce Tritan Nutri Ninja Cup. Select BOOST NO Auto-iQ™ PUREE. Remove blades from cup after blending.

5. Return soup to saucepan, then simmer until heated through.

DO NOT BLEND HOT INGREDIENTS.

CREAMY BUTTERNUT SQUASH SAUCE

Prep time: 15 minutes **Cook time:** 30 minutes
Container: 88-ounce Blender Pitcher
Makes: 6 1/2 cups

INGREDIENTS

1 tablespoon olive oil

2 cloves garlic, peeled, chopped

1 medium onion, chopped

1 1/2 pounds butternut squash,
cut in 1-inch pieces

2 teaspoons salt

1/2 teaspoon ground black pepper

1/2 teaspoon ground nutmeg

1/2 teaspoon dried thyme

4 cups low-sodium
vegetable broth

1/2 pound silken tofu

DIRECTIONS

1. Place oil, garlic, and onion into a 5-quart saucepan over medium-low heat. Cook for 5 minutes.

2. Add butternut squash, salt, pepper, nutmeg, thyme, and broth to saucepan. Bring to a boil, then reduce heat to medium-low and cook for 20 minutes.

3. Remove sauce from heat and cool to room temperature.

4. Place cooled mixture and tofu into the 88-ounce Blender Pitcher. Select BOOST YES Auto-iQ™ PUREE.

5. Return sauce to saucepan, then simmer until heated through.

DO NOT BLEND HOT INGREDIENTS.

SAUSAGE GRAVY

Prep time: 15 minutes **Cook time:** 55 minutes
Container: 88-ounce Blender Pitcher
Makes: 10 cups

INGREDIENTS

2 pounds lean pork,
cut in 1-inch pieces

1 medium onion, chopped

2 cloves garlic, peeled, chopped

1 tablespoon dried basil

1 tablespoon dried oregano

1 teaspoon crushed red pepper

¾ teaspoon fennel seed

2 teaspoons salt

1 teaspoon ground black pepper

1 tablespoon canola oil

1 can (28 ounces)
crushed tomatoes

4 cups low-sodium chicken broth

1 can (6 ounces) tomato paste

1 tablespoon sugar

3 bay leaves

DIRECTIONS

1. Place pork, onion, garlic, basil, oregano, crushed red pepper, fennel, salt, and pepper into the 88-ounce Blender Pitcher. Select BOOST YES Auto-iQ™ PUREE.

2. Add oil and pork mixture to a 5-quart saucepan over medium heat. Cook for 10 minutes, or until pork mixture is cooked through.

3. Add crushed tomatoes, broth, tomato paste, sugar, and bay leaves to saucepan. Bring to a boil, then reduce heat to medium-low and cook for 45 minutes.

DO NOT BLEND HOT INGREDIENTS.

ASIAN SWEET & SOUR SAUCE

Prep time: 10 minutes
Container: 24-ounce Tritan™ Nutri Ninja® Cup
Makes: 2 cups

INGREDIENTS

1 can (8 ounces) crushed pineapple

½ cup ketchup

⅓ cup rice wine vinegar

¼ cup low-sodium soy sauce

¼ cup sugar

2 tablespoons sesame oil

2 cloves garlic, peeled

1-inch piece fresh ginger, peeled

½ teaspoon salt

½ teaspoon ground black pepper

DIRECTIONS

1. Place all ingredients into the 24-ounce Tritan Nutri Ninja Cup in the order listed.

2. Select BOOST YES Auto-iQ™ PUREE.

3. Remove blades from cup after blending.

SPINACH ARTICHOKE ALFREDO SAUCE

Prep time: 15 minutes **Cook time:** 30 minutes
Container: 88-ounce Blender Pitcher
Makes: 9 cups

INGREDIENTS

3 tablespoons unsalted butter

2 cloves garlic, peeled, chopped

1 large onion, chopped

⅓ cup all-purpose flour

2 teaspoons salt

1 teaspoon ground black pepper

1 can (14 ounces)
artichoke hearts, drained

1 pound baby spinach

4 cups low-sodium
vegetable broth

2 cups grated Parmesan cheese

½ cup sour cream

DIRECTIONS

1. Place butter, garlic, and onion into a 5-quart saucepan over medium-low heat. Cook for 5 minutes.

2. Add flour, salt, and pepper, and stir to incorporate. Add artichoke hearts, spinach, and broth. Bring to a boil, then reduce heat to medium-low and cook for 20 minutes.

3. Remove from heat and cool to room temperature.

4. Place cooled mixture into the 88-ounce Blender Pitcher. Select BOOST NO Auto-iQ™ PUREE.

5. Return sauce to saucepan, add cheese and sour cream, then simmer until heated through.

DO NOT BLEND HOT INGREDIENTS.

MOJO MARINADE

Prep time: 10 minutes
Container: 24-ounce Tritan™ Nutri Ninja® Cup
Makes: 2 ½ cups

INGREDIENTS

1 orange, peeled,
cut in half, seeds removed

¾ cup water

½ cup olive oil

¼ cup white vinegar

1 medium shallot, peeled

2 cloves garlic, peeled

1 teaspoon dried oregano

1 ½ teaspoons ground cumin

⅓ cup fresh cilantro leaves

1 jalapeño pepper,
cut in half, seeds removed

½ teaspoon salt

½ teaspoon ground black pepper

DIRECTIONS

1. Place all ingredients into the 24-ounce Tritan Nutri Ninja Cup in the order listed.

2. Select BOOST YES Auto-iQ™ PUREE.

3. Remove blades from cup after blending.

AVOCADO WATERCRESS SALAD DRESSING

Prep time: 10 minutes
Container: 24-ounce Tritan™ Nutri Ninja® Cup
Makes: 2 cups

INGREDIENTS

1 avocado, pit removed, peeled

1 ½ cups watercress

⅔ cup olive oil

½ cup water

⅓ cup white vinegar

2 tablespoons Dijon mustard

2 cloves garlic, peeled

½ teaspoon salt

½ teaspoon ground black pepper

DIRECTIONS

1. Place all ingredients into the 24-ounce Tritan Nutri Ninja Cup in the order listed.

2. Select BOOST YES Auto-iQ™ PUREE.

3. Remove blades from cup after blending.

FROZEN MOJITO

Prep time: 5 minutes
Container: 88-ounce Blender Pitcher
Makes: 8 (10-ounce) servings

INGREDIENTS

1 cup simple syrup

Juice of 8 limes

1 bunch fresh mint, stems removed

2 cups white rum

8 cups ice

DIRECTIONS

1. Place all ingredients into the 88-ounce Blender Pitcher in the order listed.

2. Select BOOST YES Auto-iQ™ FROZEN DRINK.

PEACH, GREEN TEA & WHITE PEPPER DAIQUIRI

Prep time: 15 minutes **Cool time:** 1 1/2 hours
Container: 88-ounce Blender Pitcher
Makes: 8 (8-ounce) servings

INGREDIENTS

WHITE PEPPER GREEN TEA SYRUP

3/4 cup water

3/4 cup sugar

3 green tea bags

2 tablespoons whole white peppercorns

DAIQUIRI

1 1/2 cups White Pepper Green Tea Syrup

1/2 cup white rum

6 limes, juiced (6 ounces), zest reserved for garnish

3 ripe peaches, roughly cubed (about 4 cups)

6 cups ice

DIRECTIONS

1. To make the White Pepper-Green Tea Syrup, combine water and sugar in a saucepan. Bring to a boil, then reduce heat and simmer gently until sugar is dissolved. Add tea bags and whole peppercorns and let cool completely for 1 1/2 hours. Strain and refrigerate syrup for up to 2 weeks.

2. Add cooled syrup, rum, lime juice, peaches, and ice to the 88-ounce Pitcher and select BOOST YES Auto-iQ™ FROZEN DRINK.

3. Garnish with lime zest.

DO NOT BLEND HOT INGREDIENTS.

TROPICAL COOLER

Prep time: 10 minutes
Container: 88-ounce Blender Pitcher, 24-ounce Tritan™ Nutri Ninja® Cup
Makes: 7 (8-ounce) servings

INGREDIENTS

1 cup pineapple chunks

½ jalapeño pepper, seeds removed

½-inch piece fresh ginger, peeled

⅓ English cucumber, peeled, cut in quarters

Juice of 1½ limes

1½ cups coconut water

½ cups silver tequila

3 tablespoons agave nectar

¼ teaspoon ground cardamom

3½ cups frozen mango chunks

1½ cups ice

GARNISH

¼ cup unsweetened coconut flakes

¼ heaping teaspoon cayenne pepper

Lime wedge

8 unpeeled cucumber slices

DIRECTIONS

1. Place all ingredients, except those for the garnish, into the 88-ounce Blender Pitcher in the order listed.

2. Select BOOST YES Auto-iQ™ FROZEN DRINK.

3. To make the garnish, place coconut flakes and cayenne pepper in the 24-ounce Tritan Nutri Ninja Cup. PULSE 10 times.

4. Remove blades from cup after blending, then pour mixture onto a flat plate. Wet rims of glasses with lime wedge, then turn them upside down in the coconut-cayenne mixture.

5. Pour the cocktail into glasses and place a cucumber slice on the rim of each.

FROZEN IRISH COFFEE

Prep time: 5 minutes
Container: 88-ounce Blender Pitcher
Makes: 8 (10-ounce) servings

INGREDIENTS

1 cup Irish cream liqueur

1 cup milk

1 cup sugar

3 cups brewed coffee, chilled

6 cups ice cubes

DIRECTIONS

1. Place all ingredients into the 88-ounce Blender Pitcher in the order listed.

2. Select BOOST YES Auto-iQ™ FROZEN DRINK.

DO NOT BLEND HOT INGREDIENTS.

FROZEN MUDSLIDE

Prep time: 5 minutes
Container: 88-ounce Blender Pitcher
Makes: 8 (10-ounce) servings

INGREDIENTS

1 cup plus 2 tablespoons (10 ounces) double-strength coffee, chilled

1 cup coffee-flavored liqueur

$3/4$ cups Irish cream liqueur

1 cup whole milk

$1/2$ cup chocolate syrup

10 cups ice

DIRECTIONS

1. Place all ingredients into the 88-ounce Blender Pitcher in the order listed.

2. Select BOOST YES Auto-iQ™ FROZEN DRINK.

DO NOT BLEND HOT INGREDIENTS.

FROZEN MOCHA-TINI

Prep time: 4 minutes
Container: 88-ounce Blender Pitcher
Makes: 10 (8-ounce) servings

INGREDIENTS

1 cup semisweet chocolate chips

1 cup half & half

1 cup vanilla vodka

$^1/_2$ cup coffee liqueur

1 cup coffee, chilled

6 cups ice

DIRECTIONS

1. Place all ingredients into the 88-ounce Blender Pitcher in the order listed.

2. Select BOOST YES Auto-iQ™ FROZEN DRINK.

DO NOT BLEND HOT INGREDIENTS.

FROZEN SANGRIA

Prep time: 5 minutes
Container: 88-ounce Blender Pitcher
Makes: 8 (8-ounce) servings

INGREDIENTS

³/₄ cup pineapple chunks

1 lemon, peeled, cut in half, seeds removed

1 orange, peeled, cut in half, seeds removed

2 cups sweet red wine

²/₃ cup brandy

³/₄ cup frozen strawberries

³/₄ cup frozen peach slices

5 cups ice

DIRECTIONS

1. Place all ingredients into the 88-ounce Blender Pitcher in the order listed.

2. Select BOOST YES Auto-iQ™ FROZEN DRINK.

ICED ORANGE CHOCOLATE BLAST

Prep time: 5 minutes
Container: 24-ounce Tritan™ Nutri Ninja® Cup
Makes: 2 (12-ounce) servings

INGREDIENTS

2 oranges, peeled, cut in quarters, seeds removed

⅓ cup nonfat milk

1 ½ teaspoons honey

¼ teaspoon ground cinnamon

2 teaspoons unsweetened cocoa powder

2 cups vanilla frozen yogurt

DIRECTIONS

1. Place all ingredients into the 24-ounce Tritan Nutri Ninja Cup in the order listed.

2. Select BOOST YES Auto-iQ™ SMOOTHIE.

3. Remove blades from cup after blending.

ICED COCONUT CHAI LATTE

Prep time: 5 minutes
Container: 24-ounce Tritan™ Nutri Ninja® Cup
Makes: 2 (10-ounce) servings

INGREDIENTS

$\frac{1}{2}$ cup plus 1 tablespoon
(5 ounces) double-strength
coffee, chilled

$\frac{1}{2}$ teaspoon ground cinnamon

$\frac{1}{4}$ teaspoon ground nutmeg

$\frac{1}{2}$ teaspoon ground ginger

$\frac{1}{2}$ teaspoon ground cardamom

$\frac{3}{4}$ cup coconut milk beverage

2 tablespoons vanilla syrup

2 cups ice

DIRECTIONS

1. Place all ingredients into the 24-ounce Tritan Nutri Ninja Cup in the order listed.

2. Select BOOST NO Auto-iQ™ SMOOTHIE.

3. Remove blades from cup after blending.

DO NOT BLEND HOT INGREDIENTS.

NINJA®
FREDDO

Prep time: 5 minutes
Container: 24-ounce Tritan™ Nutri Ninja® Cup
Makes: 2 (10-ounce) servings

INGREDIENTS

1 ½ cups brewed coffee, chilled

¼ cup maple syrup

½ cup ice

DIRECTIONS

1. Place all ingredients into the 24-ounce Tritan Nutri Ninja Cup in the order listed.

2. Select BOOST NO Auto-iQ™ SMOOTHIE.

DO NOT BLEND HOT INGREDIENTS.

THAI FROZEN COFFEE

Prep time: 5 minutes
Container: 88-ounce Blender Pitcher
Makes: 7 (8-ounce) servings

INGREDIENTS

2 cups double-strength coffee, chilled

$3/4$ cup lowfat milk

$3/4$ cup sweetened condensed milk

6 cups ice

DIRECTIONS

1. Place all ingredients into the 88-ounce Blender Pitcher in the order listed.

2. Select BOOST YES Auto-iQ™ FROZEN DRINK.

DO NOT BLEND HOT INGREDIENTS.

FROZEN BANANA COFFEE ALMOND MILK

Prep time: 5 minutes
Container: 88-ounce Blender Pitcher
Makes: 8 (8-ounce) servings

INGREDIENTS

3 cups almond milk

3 cups brewed coffee, chilled

3 ripe bananas, cut in half

3 cups ice

DIRECTIONS

1. Place all ingredients into the 88-ounce Blender Pitcher in the order listed.

2. Select BOOST NO Auto-iQ™ FROZEN DRINK.

DO NOT BLEND HOT INGREDIENTS.

STRAWBERRIES & CREAM MILKSHAKE

Prep time: 5 minutes
Container: 24-ounce Tritan™ Nutri Ninja® Cup
Makes: 2 (9-ounce) servings

INGREDIENTS

1 cup strawberries, hulled

1 cup milk

$\frac{1}{2}$ teaspoon vanilla extract

1 $\frac{3}{4}$ cups strawberry ice cream

DIRECTIONS

1. Place all ingredients into the 24-ounce Tritan Nutri Ninja Cup in the order listed.

2. Select BOOST NO Auto-iQ™ SMOOTHIE.

3. Remove blades from cup after blending.

MANGO LASSI

Prep time: 5 minutes
Container: 88-ounce Blender Pitcher
Makes: 8 (10-ounce) servings

INGREDIENTS

3 cups coconut milk, filtered, from a carton

1/4 cup honey

2 teaspoons ground cardamom, plus more for garnish

4 cups nonfat vanilla frozen yogurt

4 cups frozen mango chunks

DIRECTIONS

1. Place all ingredients into the 88-ounce Blender Pitcher in the order listed.

2. Select BOOST YES Auto-iQ™ FROZEN DRINK.

3. Garnish each serving with cardamom.

MOCHA NINJACCINO™

Prep time: 5 minutes
Container: 24-ounce Tritan™ Nutri Ninja® Cup
Makes: 2 (8-ounce) servings

INGREDIENTS

½ cup double-strength
brewed coffee, chilled

¼ cup 1% milk

¼ cup chocolate syrup,
plus more for garnish

3 cups ice

Whipped cream, for garnish

DIRECTIONS

1. Place all ingredients, except whipped cream, into the
   24-ounce Tritan Nutri Ninja Cup in the order listed.

2. Select BOOST NO Auto-iQ™ SMOOTHIE.

3. Remove blades from cup after blending.

4. Divide between 2 glasses, top with whipped cream, and
   drizzle with additional chocolate syrup.

DO NOT BLEND HOT INGREDIENTS.

SOUTH OF THE BORDER FROZEN COFFEE

Prep time: 5 minutes
Container: 24-ounce Tritan™ Nutri Ninja® Cup
Makes: 2 (8-ounce) servings

INGREDIENTS

³/₄ cup brewed coffee, chilled

¹/₄ teaspoon cayenne pepper

¹/₂ teaspoon ground cinnamon

2 ¹/₂ cups chocolate ice cream

DIRECTIONS

1. Place all ingredients into the 24-ounce Tritan Nutri Ninja Cup in the order listed.

2. Select BOOST NO Auto-iQ™ SMOOTHIE.

3. Remove blades from cup after blending.

DO NOT BLEND HOT INGREDIENTS.

SALTED CARAMEL NUT FROZEN COFFEE

Prep time: 5 minutes
Container: 88-ounce Blender Pitcher
Makes: 10 (8-ounce) servings

INGREDIENTS

$^1/_3$ cup dry-roasted
salted peanuts

$^3/_4$ cup caramel flavored creamer

1 cup caramel sauce

3 cups brewed coffee, chilled

7 cups ice

DIRECTIONS

1. Place all ingredients into the 88-ounce Blender Pitcher in the order listed.

2. Select BOOST YES Auto-iQ™ FROZEN DRINK.

DO NOT BLEND HOT INGREDIENTS.

MINT CHOCOLATE CHIP SHAKE

Prep time: 5 minutes
Container: 24-ounce Tritan™ Nutri Ninja® Cup
Makes: 2 (10-ounce) servings

INGREDIENTS

4 mint chocolate cream sandwich cookies

¼ cup chocolate chips

¾ cup milk

¼ teaspoon peppermint extract

2 cups vanilla ice cream

DIRECTIONS

1. Place all ingredients into the 24-ounce Tritan Nutri Ninja Cup in the order listed.

2. Select BOOST NO Auto-iQ™ SMOOTHIE.

3. Remove blades from cup after blending.

ROCKY ROAD MILKSHAKE

Prep time: 5 minutes
Container: 24-ounce Tritan™ Nutri Ninja® Cup
Makes: 2 (10-ounce) servings

INGREDIENTS

¼ cup pecan halves

¼ cup mini marshmallows

1 cup milk

1 tablespoon cocoa powder

2 cups vanilla ice cream

DIRECTIONS

1. Place all ingredients into the 24-ounce Tritan Nutri Ninja Cup in the order listed.

2. Select BOOST NO Auto-iQ™ SMOOTHIE.

3. Remove blades from cup after blending.

S'MORES FROZEN COFFEE

Prep time: 5 minutes
Container: 88-ounce Blender Pitcher
Makes: 8 (8-ounce) servings

INGREDIENTS

4 full graham crackers

1/2 cup semisweet chocolate chips

1 cup mini marshmallows

2 1/2 cups brewed coffee, chilled

1 1/2 cups chocolate almond milk

6 cups ice

DIRECTIONS

1. Place all ingredients into the 88-ounce Blender Pitcher in the order listed.

2. Select BOOST YES Auto-iQ™ FROZEN DRINK.

DO NOT BLEND HOT INGREDIENTS.

STRAWBERRY CITRUS SLUSH

Prep time: 5 minutes **Freeze time:** 8 hours
Container: 88-ounce Blender Pitcher
Makes: 6 (8-ounce) servings

INGREDIENTS

STRAWBERRY ICE CUBES

5 cups strawberries, hulled

2 limes, peeled, cut in half, seeds removed

⅓ cup honey

4 cups ice

SLUSH

Strawberry ice cubes

1 cup orange juice

DIRECTIONS

1. Place all ingredients for the strawberry ice cubes into the 88-ounce Blender Pitcher in the order listed.

2. Select BOOST YES Auto-iQ™ PUREE.

3. Pour into ice cube trays and freeze 8 hours or overnight.

4. To make the slush, place strawberry ice cubes and orange juice into the 88-ounce Blender Pitcher and select BOOST NO Auto-iQ™ TOTAL CRUSH.

5. Add additional orange juice through the pour spout while blending if necessary.

VANILLA ALMOND FROZEN COFFEE

Prep time: 5 minutes
Container: 24-ounce Tritan™ Nutri Ninja® Cup
Makes: 2 (12-ounce) servings

INGREDIENTS

1 cup brewed coffee, chilled

⅛ teaspoon almond extract

3 tablespoons almond butter

2 cups vanilla ice cream

DIRECTIONS

1. Place all ingredients into the 24-ounce Tritan Nutri Ninja Cup in the order listed.

2. Select BOOST NO Auto-iQ™ SMOOTHIE.

3. Remove blades from cup after blending.

DO NOT BLEND HOT INGREDIENTS.

BLUEBERRY VANILLA CHIP ICE CREAM

Prep time: 5 minutes
Container: 88-ounce Blender Pitcher
Makes: 6 (4-ounce) servings

INGREDIENTS

$^1/_2$ cup white chocolate chips

$^3/_4$ cup light cream

1 teaspoon vanilla extract

2 tablespoons lemon juice

3 cups frozen blueberries

DIRECTIONS

1. Place all ingredients into the 88-ounce Blender Pitcher in the order listed.

2. Select BOOST YES Auto-iQ™ PUREE.

STRAWBERRY CHEESECAKE IN A GLASS

Prep time: 4 minutes
Container: 24-ounce Tritan™ Nutri Ninja® Cup
Makes: 2 (8-ounce) servings

INGREDIENTS

1 full graham cracker

1 cup milk

¼ cup cream cheese

1 cup vanilla ice cream

¾ cup frozen strawberries

DIRECTIONS

1. Place all ingredients into the 24-ounce Tritan Nutri Ninja Cup in the order listed.

2. Select BOOST NO Auto-iQ™ SMOOTHIE.

3. Remove blades from cup after blending.

FROZEN BANANA SPLIT

Prep time: 5 minutes
Container: 88-ounce Blender Pitcher
Makes: 8 (8-ounce) servings

INGREDIENTS

$\frac{1}{2}$ cup walnut halves

$\frac{1}{2}$ cup mini semisweet chocolate chips

2 cups strawberries, hulled

2 ripe bananas

2 cups milk

4 cups vanilla ice cream

Whipped cream, for garnish

Maraschino cherries, for garnish

Caramel and chocolate sauce, for garnish

DIRECTIONS

1. Place all ingredients into the 88-ounce Blender Pitcher in the order listed.

2. Select BOOST NO Auto-iQ™ FROZEN DRINK.

3. Top each serving with whipped cream and a cherry, then drizzle with caramel and chocolate sauces.

GRAPEFRUIT GRANITA

Prep time: 5 minutes **Freeze time:** 8 hours
Container: 88-ounce Blender Pitcher
Makes: 4 (10-ounce) servings

INGREDIENTS

4 pink grapefruits, peeled,
cut in quarters, seeds removed

1 ½ cups water

⅓ cup honey

DIRECTIONS

1. Place all ingredients into the 88-ounce Blender Pitcher in the order listed.

2. Select BOOST YES Auto-iQ™ PUREE.

3. Pour mixture into 3 standard ice cube trays, equally distributing between trays. Freeze for 8 hours or overnight.

4. Remove frozen grapefruit cubes and place into the 88-ounce Blender Pitcher.

5. Select BOOST YES Auto-iQ TOTAL CRUSH.

CHERRY POM GRANITA

Prep time: 5 minutes **Freeze time:** 8 hours
Container: 88-ounce Blender Pitcher
Makes: 10 (8-ounce) servings

INGREDIENTS

4 cups pomegranate juice

¼ cup agave nectar

5 cups frozen dark sweet cherries

DIRECTIONS

1. Place all ingredients into the 88-ounce Blender Pitcher in the order listed.

2. Select BOOST YES Auto-iQ™ PUREE. Run the program twice for the finest texture.

3. Pour mixture into 4 standard ice cube trays, equally distributing between trays. Freeze for 8 hours or overnight.

4. Remove frozen cubes and place into the 88-ounce Blender Pitcher, in batches.

5. Select BOOST YES Auto-iQ TOTAL CRUSH.

THAI CHAI GRANITA

Prep time: 5 minutes   **Freeze time:** 8 hours
Container: 88-ounce Blender Pitcher
Makes: 8 (8-ounce) servings

INGREDIENTS

5 cups brewed Thai tea, chilled

1 can (14 ounces) sweetened condensed milk

1 can (12 ounces) evaporated milk

1 tablespoon vanilla extract

DIRECTIONS

1. Place all ingredients into the 88-ounce Blender Pitcher in the order listed.

2. PULSE 4 times.

3. Pour mixture into 4 standard ice cube trays, equally distributing between trays. Freeze for 8 hours or overnight.

4. Remove frozen cubes and place into the 88-ounce Blender Pitcher, in batches.

5. Select BOOST YES Auto-iQ™ TOTAL CRUSH.

DO NOT BLEND HOT INGREDIENTS.

TROPICAL FRESH FRUIT ICE POPS

Prep time: 5 minutes **Freeze time:** 8 hours
Container: 24-ounce Tritan™ Nutri Ninja® Cup
Makes: 4 ice pops

INGREDIENTS

1 cup mango chunks

2 cups pineapple chunks

2 tablespoons agave nectar

DIRECTIONS

1. Place all ingredients into the 24-ounce Tritan Nutri Ninja Cup in the order listed.

2. Select BOOST YES Auto-iQ™ PUREE. Remove blades from cup after blending.

3. Pour mixture into ice pop molds, and freeze for 8 hours or overnight.

FUDGY ICE POPS

Prep time: 15 minutes   **Cook time:** 10 minutes   **Freeze time:** 8 hours
Container: 88-ounce Blender Pitcher
Makes: 14 (3-ounce) servings

INGREDIENTS

4 cups whole milk

1 cup heavy cream

¾ cup sugar

¼ cup unsweetened cocoa

4 bars (3.5 ounces each)
dark chocolate, chopped

1 tablespoon vanilla extract

1 teaspoon salt

DIRECTIONS

1. Place milk, heavy cream, sugar, and cocoa powder into a saucepan over medium heat. Cook until sugar and cocoa powder are well combined and dissolved, about 10 minutes. Let cool.

2. Placed cooled milk mixture, chocolate, vanilla, and salt into the 88-ounce Blender Pitcher.

3. Select BOOST NO Auto-iQ™ PUREE.

4. Pour the mixture into ice pop molds, equally distributing between the molds.

5. Place the ice pop molds in the freezer for 8 hours or overnight.

DO NOT BLEND HOT INGREDIENTS.

TROPICAL RICE PUDDING ICE CREAM

Prep time: 5 minutes
Container: 88-ounce Blender Pitcher
Makes: 6 (4-ounce) servings

INGREDIENTS

$1/2$ cup light coconut milk

1 cup pre-made rice pudding

2 $1/3$ cups frozen mango chunks

1 $1/4$ cups frozen pineapple chunks

DIRECTIONS

1. Place all ingredients into the 88-ounce Blender Pitcher in the order listed.

2. Select BOOST YES Auto-iQ™ PUREE.

STRAWBERRY SNOW

Prep time: 2 minutes
Container: 88-ounce Blender Pitcher
Makes: 4 (5-ounce) servings

INGREDIENTS

4 cups frozen strawberries

DIRECTIONS

1. Place all ingredients into the 88-ounce Blender Pitcher.

4. Select BOOST YES Auto-iQ™ TOTAL CRUSH.

INDEX

FROZEN DRINKS & MILKSHAKES

Frozen Banana Coffee Almond Milk	90
Iced Coconut Chai Latte	86
Iced Orange Chocolate Blast	84
Mango Lassi	92
Mint Chocolate Chip Shake	98
Mocha Ninjaccino™	95
Ninja® Freddo	87
Rocky Road Milkshake	101
Salted Caramel Nut Frozen Coffee	97
S'mores Frozen Coffee	102
South of the Border Frozen Coffee	96
Strawberries & Cream Milkshake	91
Strawberry Citrus Slush	103
Thai Frozen Coffee	89
Vanilla Almond Frozen Coffee	104

DESSERTS

Blueberry Vanilla Chip Ice Cream	106
Cherry Pom Granita	112
Frozen Banana Split	109
Fudgy Ice Pops	116
Grapefruit Granita	110
Strawberry Cheesecake in a Glass	108
Strawberry Snow	118
Tropical Fresh Fruit Ice Pops	115
Tropical Rice Pudding Ice Cream	117
Thai Chai Granita	113

NOTES